A TALE FROM THE SMOKY MOUNTAINS
THE TREE THAT LOVED

Story and illustrations

by

Robert Snyder

Robert Snyder

Job 14:7

M

Math—it's not just counting 68
Moveable parts 27
Movement activities 50
Movement experiences 52
Music experiences 56
Music from your body 59
Music using CDs 59

N

New Rules for boysthat work better in early childhood settings 89

P

Parents send messages about what "real boys" do 13
Pause state to active state 4
Power spaces 35
Putting yourself in a boy's place 93

R

Ralph the "runner" 93
Rhymes, chants and finger plays 58
Roughhousing spaces 34
Running spaces 29

S

Same-sex play molds differences in behavior 18
Science for boys 45
Should we have single sex classrooms? 88
Solitary spaces 37
Steps for reducing hitting with boys 76

T

Television and other media send messages about gender 16
Toys and games reinforce ideas about gender differences 17

W

Water play spaces 31
What boys need? 95
What can I do about boys who want to play guns or swords? 82
What can I do with a bully? 77
What pushes Your buttons? 79
What you'll find in this book viii
Will "super hero" play promote violence? 83
Writing on the go 66

ISBN 978-1-7375943-3-8 (Paperback)

Copyright © 2019 Robert Snyder
All rights reserved
Second Edition

All rights reserved. No part of this publication may be reproduced, distributed, or transmitted in any form or by any means, including photocopying, recording, or other electronic or mechanical methods, without the prior written permission of the publisher. For permission requests, solicit the publisher via the address below

Robert Snyder
PO Box 725
Townsend, TN 37882
bandcsnyder@yahoo.com

It was summer and the grandchildren were spending part of their vacation with Grammy and Grampy. Reagan, Mason, and their cousin Colton loved to visit their grandparents, who lived very close to the Great Smoky Mountains National Park. Time with them always included hikes and picnics in the mountains.

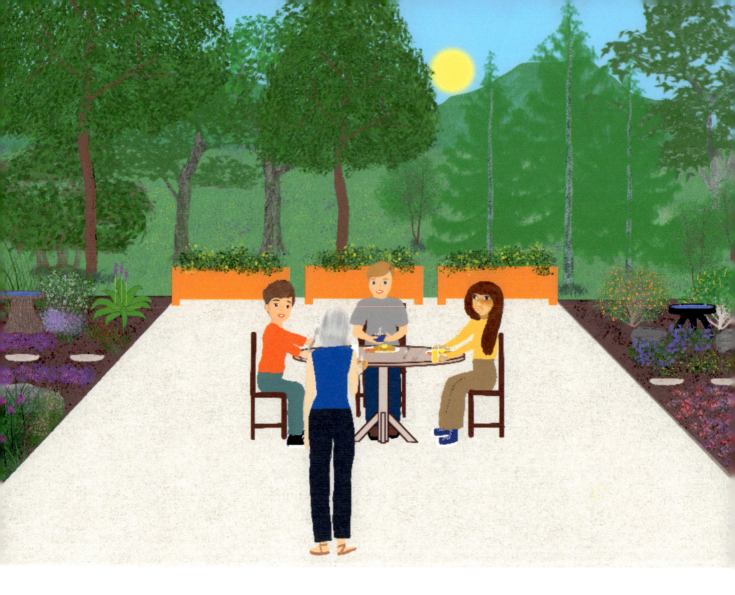

On one especially beautiful morning, while the children were enjoying their breakfast and talking with Grammy, Grampy walked onto the patio and said, "I have a great idea."

"What is it Grampy?" asked the children.

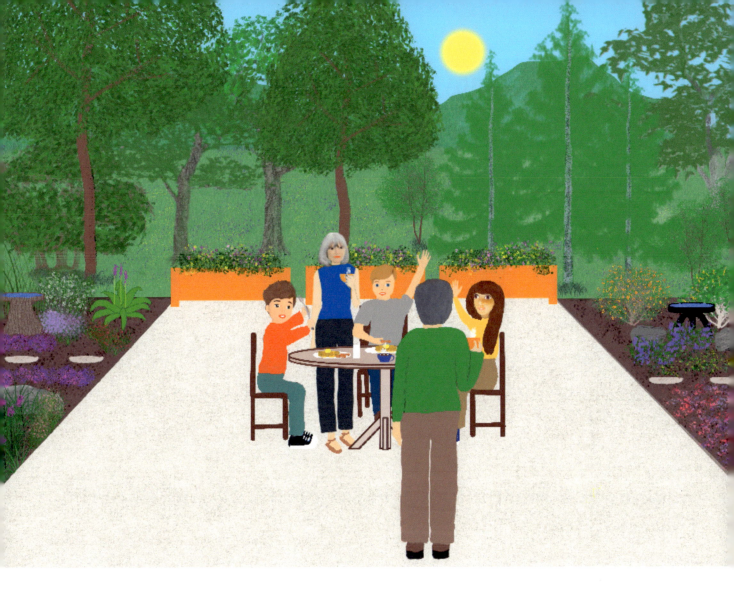

"I think we should have a picnic where there are lots of wildlife, beautiful pastures, and lush forests surrounded by spectacular mountains."

"We know where that is," replied the children. "Cades Cove! Yeah, a picnic in the Cove!"

"I hope we see a baby bear," said Reagan. "They're so cute."

"I want to see a turkey," exclaimed Mason and began strutting around the breakfast table, gobbling and bobbing his head up and down imitating the comical-looking bird.

"I know we will see deer," replied Colton, "My dad saw 129 deer while on a hayride through the Cove when he was a kid. "

Reagan and Mason looked at each other and said at the same time, "WOW, 129 deer."

"We'll leave around three thirty this afternoon and stop in Townsend to get burgers, fries and shakes," said Grampy.

"Yummy! Burgers, fries, and milkshakes," said the excited children.

Grampy's plan was a big hit.

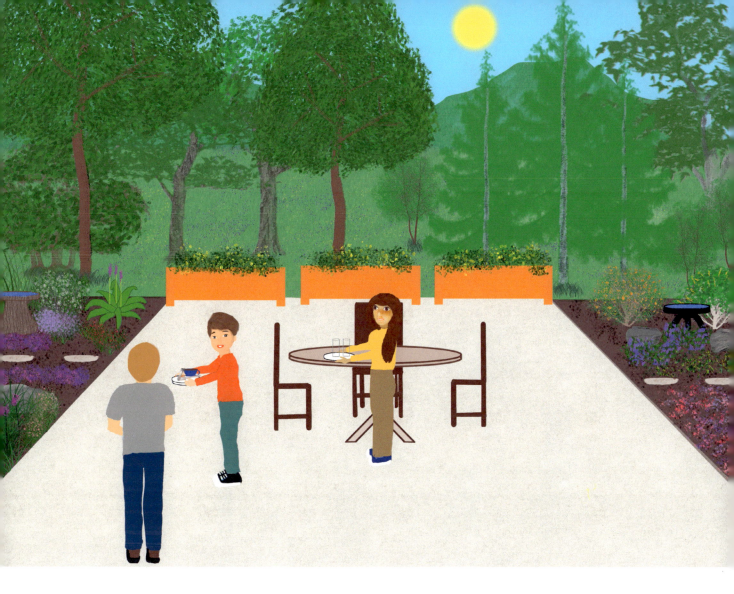

The children knew Grammy needed time to prepare for their picnic, so they cleared the table and washed the breakfast dishes.

At three thirty, everyone piled into Grampy's jeep, and off they went. They stopped at the Burger Master and purchased their food and drinks.

After a curvy ride along Laurel Creek Road, they entered Cades Cove.

The spot they chose for their picnic was under a shady tree across the road from Woody.

Woody was their favorite tree. The arrangement of several knots on Woody's trunk resembled two eyes and a nose. A large scar in the bark just below the nose formed his big smile. The leaves at the tip of a large branch that stretched out over Cades Cove Loop Road gave the appearance of a large hand, waving a big friendly hello to each visitor that passed by. Reagan gave Woody the official title "Cades Cove Greeter."

Grampy parked the jeep in the pull-off next to Woody. The grandchildren helped him remove the picnic basket and a cooler from the jeep.

As Grampy closed the tailgate on the jeep, he waved a big hello to Woody.

Reagan, Mason, and Colton sat on a log and waited patiently as Grammy laid the food out on the big red picnic blanket. She surprised everyone when she removed one of her famous strawberry pies from the picnic basket.

"Oooh, Grammy, that pie looks amazing," exclaimed Colton.

"Thank you, Colton. I hope everyone likes it."

"I'm sure they will," he replied.

Grampy thanked God for the food and the opportunity to enjoy His beautiful creation. Then, everyone dug in.

"Grampy has been doing a lot of hiking lately. You know when he hikes, he thinks up good stories. I wonder if he has a new one for us? Anyone in the mood for a story?" Grammy asked.

"Yes. Please, please tell us a story Grampy!" begged the children.

"As a matter of fact, I have a new story."

"What's the name of the story?" asked Colton.

"The title of the story is "The Tree That Loved," Grampy replied.

"It goes like this:

When Mother Maple released her seeds many years ago, three of the seeds were caught by a strong wind that carried them through Happy Valley Gap and dropped them along the bank of Abrams Creek.

Because the Smoky Mountains receives a lot of rain, especially in the spring, it's not unusual for Abrams Creek to overflow its banks and replenish the soil with minerals and nutrients.

The soil where the three maple seeds landed was so rich, the seeds quickly took root and grew to be strong, beautiful trees.

The three trees were very happy and loved providing homes for the birds, chipmunks, and squirrels. Bears would snooze in their branches, and occasionally hikers stopped and rested in the shade the trees provided.

The trees could never have imagined how their wonderful life would change due to a drought. The spring rains never came, and Abrams Creek was reduced to a slow trickle. The soil became dry and hard, lacking the moisture the trees needed to survive.

The leaves on the trees began to wilt and turn brown. They suffered terribly through the hot summer.

When summer gave way to fall and winter, the trees were grateful for the opportunity to rest. They hoped the rains would resume soon and end the drought.

With the beginning of spring, the mountains started to warm, but the spring rains still did not come, and the drought continued. Normally, the sap rose from the trees' roots and flowed through each branch and stem to feed the colorful buds that would become leaves.

But this spring, the three maple trees knew they would not be able to produce enough leaves to remain healthy. They were afraid they might even die if the rains did not come soon. They were very sad.

The tree that lived between his brother and sister said to his family, "I have thought about our situation all winter. Because we grew so close together, we put a larger demand on the soil than it can provide during the drought. The soil can support two of us but not three. I have decided to lay down my life so that you two can live. I will drop my leaves and shed my protective bark."

His brother and sister cried out, "No, no, we could not bear to live without you, brother." But the tree's love for his brother and sister was so great that he was willing to die for them.

The maple tree took one last look at the beautiful mountains and forest. Then he dropped his leaves and shed his bark.

As the weeks passed, worms and bugs attacked his unprotected trunk. The woodpeckers, looking for food, pecked large holes in the dying tree.

When strong winds swept through the valley, the tree's weak trunk broke and the tree fell to the ground.

Even though the two remaining maple trees were very sad, they began to get stronger.

Their brother's sacrifice had saved them.

The summer was ending, and once again, the forest was starting to display fall colors. The two maple trees displayed the most brilliant colors that had ever been seen in honor of their brother, the tree that loved. They were hopeful as they entered their winter sleep.

As the earth made its way around the sun, it wasn't long before the banks of Abrams Creek began to warm again. It was time to grow, produce leaves, and make sap.

When the two maple trees woke up from their winter sleep, they discovered the drought had ended and Abrams Creek was full from the spring rains. An early flood had renewed the soil, and the trees began to flourish.

The nasty old thorn bush that lived on the other side of the Creek yelled out to the two maple trees with a gruff voice, "If your brother had waited, he would still be alive today."

The two trees responded, "Hush, you mean old thorn bush. The sacrifice our brother made was a beautiful act. We would have died if not for him."

Then the maple trees looked at the spot where their brother once grew.

They could not believe what they saw, and they sang out, "Look! Look! Our brother lives."

From his old stump, a strong sapling was growing, reaching up towards the blue sky. They were amazed and full of joy and wonder.

They shouted, "Our brother who gave his life for us is alive."

Once again the three trees were happy, living a wonderful life along Abrams Creek.

And that's the end of the story."

Grammy and the grandchildren cheered.

"Oh, Grampy, I love your new story," Reagan replied as she clapped.

"Thank you, Reagan," Grampy responded with satisfaction.

"I love it, too," agreed Mason, "and I'm so happy the tree lived."

Colton was thinking and said, "The story reminds me of something I read in the Bible."

Grammy asked, "Could it be John 15:12, where Jesus taught his disciples that no greater love has a person for a friend than if he lays down his life for them?"

"That's just the verse I was trying to think of," replied Colton. "Thank you, Grammy."

"I thought of something, too," said Reagan.

"What is it?" Grammy asked.

"The tree came back to life, right?"

"That's correct," Grammy replied.

"Well, the loving tree was just like Jesus. He laid down his life to save his brothers and sisters and then came back to life."

"Excellent," Grampy said, "I was hoping the story would help you kids understand the great sacrifice Jesus made for all of us. You guys really have your thinking caps on today."

Mason, always the jokester, put a large catalpa leaf on his head and asked, "What's a thinking cap?"

Everyone burst out laughing.

Mason continued, "Grampy, can we get something to drink on the way home? Storytelling makes me thirsty."

"When Grampy throws away the trash at the Ranger Station, we'll get some sodas from the Cades Cove Camp store," said Grammy.

Grampy nodded in agreement.

"The sun is starting to set below the mountaintops. I think we better gather everything up and head for home before it gets too dark," Grampy announced.

Grammy and the grandchildren got into the jeep while Grampy inspected the area one last time to make sure they had not left any trash behind.

Grampy stopped at the ranger station and put the trash bag in the dumpster, while the children ran into the store to purchase their sodas.

As they drove along Laurel Creek, they sang songs and enjoyed their sodas.

When Grampy exited the highway and started up the lane that led to their house, Colton remarked, "I sure had a great time. This is a day I'll always remember."

"Me, too!" exclaimed Reagan.

Mason, taking his last big sip of soda, let out a giant burp and said, "Me, three.

Woody is a real tree. He lives in Cades Cove along the 11-mile loop road. The next time you're in the Cove, be sure to look for him. During the summer, a lot of vines grow around Woody's face and make it more difficult to see his eyes, nose, and mouth. So look closely.

Here is a hint to help you find him.

On the return side of loop, past the gift shop, look for a "20-MPH" sign on the right-hand side of the road. As you start down the hill, Woody will be on the right side of the road.

Woody will be waving to you, so be sure to tell him hello.

About the Author

Robert Snyder was born in Southern Indiana and grew up on a small farm. He served four years in the US Air Force followed by a 32-year career with an electric utility. Shortly after he retired, he moved to Townsend, Tennessee with his wife, Charlotte. They have two children and six grandchildren.

Titles of other books written by Robert are:

A Tale From The Smoky Mountains Brewster's Story
A Tale From The Smoky Mountains The Miracle
A Tale From The Smoky Mountains Powder
Max In The Mountains The Snake

Made in the USA
Columbia, SC
16 April 2024

34253338R00024